Git for Developers

A Comprehensive Guide to Version Control for Collaborative Development

Written by

Julie Smith

Your feedback is invaluable to me!

If you found this book helpful in any way, please take a moment to leave your review here on Amazon . Your thoughts and experiences will help other readers make informed decisions and contribute to the ongoing improvement of this work.

Table of contents

Preface

Tired of losing your work? Frustrated with merging conflicts? Confused about the tangled web of Git commands?

You're not alone. Many developers have struggled with version control, especially when working in teams. But fear not, for we've crafted a comprehensive guide to help you master Git and streamline your development workflow.

Imagine a world where you can effortlessly track changes to your code, collaborate seamlessly with your team, and experiment fearlessly without the risk of losing your work. This is the power of Git.

In this book, we'll take you on a journey through the intricacies of Git, from the fundamental concepts to advanced techniques. We'll guide you through real-world examples, practical exercises, and clear explanations to ensure you grasp every aspect of this powerful tool.

Why Git?

Git is more than just a version control system; it's a collaborative tool that empowers developers to work efficiently and effectively. With Git, you can:

- Track Changes: See the evolution of your code over time.
- Collaborate Seamlessly: Work with others on the same project, even from different locations.
- Experiment Fearlessly: Create and merge branches to try out new ideas without affecting the main codebase.
- Recover from Mistakes: Easily revert to previous versions of your code.

- Manage Complex Projects: Organize and maintain large, complex projects.

What You'll Learn:

- Git Basics: Master the core concepts of Git, including repositories, commits, branches, and merging.
- Advanced Git Techniques: Explore advanced techniques like rebasing, cherry-picking, and interactive rebasing.
- Collaborative Development: Learn how to work effectively with teams using Git's powerful collaboration features.
- Best Practices: Discover best practices for writing clear commit messages, resolving merge conflicts, and maintaining a clean Git history.
- Real-World Examples: Understand how Git is used in real-world projects, from small-scale personal projects to large-scale enterprise applications.

Whether you're a beginner or an experienced developer, this book will equip you with the knowledge and skills to become a Git expert. So, let's dive in and unlock the full potential of Git!

Part I
Git Fundamentals

Chapter 1: Introduction to Version Control

1.1 What is Version Control?

Version control is a system that tracks changes made to a set of files over time. It allows you to manage and coordinate changes to your codebase efficiently, especially when working with a team. Think of it as a time machine for your code, enabling you to:

- Track Changes: See exactly what changes were made, when, and by whom.
- Revert to Previous Versions: Roll back to an earlier version if needed.
- Collaborate Effectively: Work on the same codebase with multiple people without conflicts.
- Experiment Fearlessly: Create different versions of your code to try out new ideas.
- Manage Large Projects: Organize and maintain complex projects with ease.

Why Use Version Control?

- Accident Prevention: Mitigate the risk of accidental data loss or corruption.
- Efficient Collaboration: Facilitate teamwork and avoid conflicts.
- Improved Code Quality: Enable code reviews and better collaboration.
- Simplified Project Management: Streamline the development process.
- Enhanced Productivity: Save time and effort by automating tasks.

Key Concepts in Version Control

- Repository: A central storage location for your project's files.
- Commit: A snapshot of your project at a specific point in time.
- Branch: A separate line of development, allowing you to work on different features or bug fixes independently.
- Merge: Combining changes from one branch into another.
- Checkout: Switching between different versions or branches of your code.

By understanding these core concepts, you'll be well-equipped to leverage the power of version control in your development projects.

1.2 Why Use Version Control?

Version control is a powerful tool that offers a multitude of benefits for developers, both individually and in collaborative teams. Here are some compelling reasons why you should consider using version control:

1. Accident Prevention

- Undo Mistakes: If you accidentally make a mistake, you can easily revert to a previous version of your code.
- Recover Lost Work: In case of accidental deletion or corruption, you can restore lost files from previous versions.

2. Efficient Collaboration

- Parallel Development: Multiple developers can work on different parts of a project simultaneously without interfering with each other.
- Conflict Resolution: Version control systems help identify and resolve conflicts when multiple people modify the same files.

- Code Review: Team members can review each other's code, ensuring quality and consistency.

3. Improved Code Quality

- Experimentation: You can experiment with different approaches without fear of breaking the main codebase.
- Code History: Track the evolution of your code over time, making it easier to identify and fix bugs.
- Learning Opportunities: Analyze past changes to learn from mistakes and improve future development.

4. Simplified Project Management

- Organization: Version control systems help you organize your project's files and history.
- Release Management: Easily manage different software releases and track changes between versions.
- Bug Tracking: Link code changes to specific bug fixes or feature implementations.

5. Enhanced Productivity

- Automation: Version control systems automate many tasks, such as backups, versioning, and merging.
- Time-Saving: Quickly switch between different versions and branches.
- Reduced Stress: Avoid the anxiety of losing work or dealing with complex merge conflicts.

By embracing version control, you can significantly enhance your development workflow, improve code quality, and collaborate more effectively with your team.

1.3 A Brief History of Version Control Systems

Version control systems have evolved over decades to meet the growing needs of software development. Let's take a brief look at some of the major milestones in their history:

Early Version Control Systems

- Local Version Control Systems:
    - Simple systems like RCS (Revision Control System) and SCCS (Source Code Control System) were used to track changes to files on a single machine.
    - These systems were limited to local use and lacked features like branching and merging.

Centralized Version Control Systems

- CVS (Concurrent Versions System):
    - One of the first widely adopted centralized version control systems.
    - It allowed multiple developers to work on a shared codebase, but it struggled with complex workflows and performance issues.
- SVN (Subversion):
    - A successor to CVS, SVN offered improved performance, better branching and merging capabilities, and a more user-friendly interface.
    - However, it still relied on a centralized server, which could be a single point of failure.

Distributed Version Control Systems

- Git:
    - A powerful and flexible distributed version control system.
    - Each developer has a complete copy of the repository, including its history.

- This decentralized approach enables efficient collaboration, offline work, and complex branching and merging strategies.
- Git has become the industry standard for version control due to its versatility and robustness.

Other notable distributed version control systems include:

- Mercurial: A fast and efficient system with a strong focus on user experience.
- Bazaar: A highly customizable and flexible system with a wide range of features.

As technology continues to advance, version control systems will undoubtedly evolve to meet the changing needs of software development. By understanding the historical context of version control, you can better appreciate the power and flexibility of modern systems like Git.

1.4 Introducing Git: A Decentralized Approach

Git is a powerful, distributed version control system that has revolutionized the way software is developed. Unlike centralized systems like SVN, Git allows each developer to have a complete copy of the repository, including its history. This decentralized approach offers several advantages:

Key Features of Git:

- Distributed Nature: Every developer has a complete copy of the repository, enabling offline work and faster operations.
- Branching and Merging: Git makes it easy to create and merge branches, allowing for parallel development and experimentation.

- Staging Area: A staging area allows you to prepare changes before committing them, giving you fine-grained control over your commits.
- Strong Commit History: Git's commit history is highly detailed, making it easy to track changes and revert to previous versions.
- Efficient Performance: Git is optimized for speed, especially when working with large repositories.

How Git Works:

1. Create a Repository: Initialize a new Git repository or clone an existing one.
2. Stage Changes: Add specific files or changes to the staging area.
3. Commit Changes: Create a snapshot of the staged changes and store it in the repository's history.
4. Branching: Create new branches to work on specific features or bug fixes.
5. Merging: Combine changes from different branches.
6. Pushing and Pulling: Share changes with remote repositories.

Why Choose Git?

- Flexibility: Git's decentralized nature offers unparalleled flexibility and freedom.
- Efficiency: It's optimized for speed and performance, even with large projects.
- Powerful Features: Branching, merging, and other advanced features make Git a versatile tool.
- Strong Community: A large and active community provides extensive support and resources.

By understanding the fundamental concepts of Git, you can harness its power to streamline your development workflow and collaborate effectively with others.

Chapter 2: Getting Started with Git

2.1 Installing Git

Git is available for various operating systems, including Windows, macOS, and Linux. Here's a general guide on how to install Git:

Windows

1. Download the Installer: Visit the official Git website (https://git-scm.com/) and download the latest installer for Windows.
2. Run the Installer: Double-click the downloaded installer and follow the on-screen instructions.
3. Customize Installation: During the installation process, you can customize options like the default text editor and terminal emulator.
4. Finish the Installation: Click "Finish" to complete the installation.

macOS

Using Homebrew:

1. Install Homebrew: If you don't have Homebrew, install it by following the instructions on the Homebrew website.
2. Install Git: Open your terminal and run the following command:

Bash

```
brew install git
```

Using the Official Installer:

1. Download the Installer: Download the latest Git installer from the official Git website.
2. Run the Installer: Follow the on-screen instructions to complete the installation.

Linux

Using the Package Manager:

Debian/Ubuntu:

Bash

```
sudo apt-get install git
```

Fedora/CentOS:

Bash

```
sudo dnf install git
```

Compiling from Source:

If you prefer to compile Git from source, you can download the source code and follow the instructions in the INSTALL file. However, this is generally not necessary for most users.

Verifying the Installation:

After installing Git, open your terminal or command prompt and type the following command:

Bash

```
git --version
```

If Git is installed correctly, you should see the version number.

Additional Tips:

1. Configure Git: Customize Git's behavior by setting your name and email address:

Bash

```
git config --global¹ user.name "Your Name"

git config --global user.email
"your_email@example.com"
```

2. Learn Basic Commands: Start by learning essential Git commands like git init, git clone, git add, git commit, git push, and git pull.
3. Use a Git GUI: Consider using a Git GUI tool like GitKraken or SourceTree to simplify complex operations.

By following these steps and exploring Git's capabilities, you can effectively manage your code and collaborate with others.

2.2 Basic Git Configuration

Before you start using Git, it's essential to configure some basic settings. This involves setting your username and email address, which will be associated with your commits.

Setting Your User Name and Email:

1. Open your terminal or command prompt.
2. Run the following commands, replacing the placeholders with your actual information:

Bash

```
git config --global user.name "Your Name"

git config --global user.email
"your_email@example.com"
```

3.
   - ○ --global: This flag sets the configuration for all your Git repositories.

Checking Your Configuration:

To verify your configuration, run the following command:

Bash

```
git config --list
```

This will display a list of your current Git configuration settings.

Editing Your Configuration File:

You can also edit your Git configuration file directly. The default location for this file is:

- Windows: C:\Users\YourUserName\.gitconfig
- macOS/Linux: ~/.gitconfig

Open this file in a text editor and modify the user.name and user.email settings as needed.

Setting Up a Text Editor:

Git uses a text editor to open files for editing, such as when committing changes or resolving merge conflicts. You can set a default text editor using the following command:

Bash

```
git config --global core.editor "your_editor"
```

Replace your_editor with the name of your preferred text editor, such as vim, nano, or notepad.

Additional Configuration Options:

Git offers many other configuration options to customize your workflow. Some common options include:

Setting a default branch name:

Bash

```
git config --global init.defaultBranch main
```

Configuring color output:

Bash

```
git config --global color.ui true
```

Setting a specific diff tool:

Bash

```
git config --global diff.tool your_diff_tool
```

By properly configuring Git, you can ensure that your commits are correctly attributed and that your development experience is tailored to your preferences.

2.3 Creating a New Repository

A Git repository is a directory that contains all the files for a project, along with the complete history of changes. To create a new Git repository, follow these steps:

1. Choose a Directory:

- Create a New Directory: Use your file explorer or terminal to create a new directory for your project.
- Navigate to the Directory: Open your terminal and navigate to the newly created directory.

2. Initialize the Repository:

Run the git init command:

Bash

git init

- This command initializes an empty Git repository in the current directory. You'll see a new .git directory created, which contains all the necessary Git files.

3. Add Files to the Repository:

- Stage Files: Use the git add command to add specific files or all files in the directory to the staging area:

Bash

git add filename.txt

or

Bash

```
git add .
```

- The latter command adds all files in the current directory and its subdirectories.

4. Commit Changes:

- Create a Commit: Use the git commit command to create a snapshot of the staged changes:

Bash

```
git commit -m "Initial commit"
```

- Replace "Initial commit" with a descriptive message about the changes you've made.

Now, your new Git repository is ready to use. You can start making changes to your files, committing them, and tracking your project's history.

Remember:

- Always commit your changes with descriptive messages to keep track of what you've done.
- Use the git status command to check the current status of your repository, including any changes that haven't been committed.

By following these steps, you'll be able to effectively manage your projects using Git.

2.4 Initializing an Existing Directory

If you have an existing directory containing files that you want to track with Git, you can initialize a Git repository within that directory. This is useful when you have an existing project that you want to start version controlling.

Here's how to initialize an existing directory:

- Navigate to the Directory: Open your terminal or command prompt and navigate to the directory you want to initialize.
- Run the git init Command: Execute the following command:

Bash

```
git init
```

- This command creates a new .git directory within your existing directory, initializing a Git repository.

Now, you can start using Git to track changes to your files:

- Add Files: Use the git add command to stage files for commit.
- Commit Changes: Use the git commit command to create a snapshot of the staged changes.
- View Commit History: Use the git log command to view the history of your commits.

Important Note:

- Overwriting Existing Files: If you have a version control system already set up in the directory, initializing a Git repository will not overwrite the existing system. You'll need to migrate your project to Git carefully.

- Careful Migration: If you're migrating from another version control system, ensure that you understand the migration process and potential conflicts.

By following these steps, you can easily add existing projects to Git and start benefiting from its powerful features.

Chapter 3: Core Git Commands

3.1 git init: Creating a New Repository

The git init command is used to initialize a new Git repository in a specific directory. This creates a hidden .git directory that stores all the necessary metadata for version control.

To initialize a new repository:

- Create a New Directory: Use your file explorer or terminal to create a new directory for your project.
- Navigate to the Directory: Open your terminal and navigate to the newly created directory.
- Run the git init Command: Type the following command in your terminal:

Bash

```
git init
```

This command will create the .git directory in your current directory, initializing a new Git repository.

What Happens When You Run git init?

- Creates a .git Directory: This directory contains all the necessary files for Git to track changes, including the repository's history, branches, and configuration settings.
- Initializes the Repository: Sets up the initial state of the repository, ready for you to start adding and committing files.

Once you've initialized a repository, you can start adding files to it and tracking changes using other Git commands.

3.2 git clone: Cloning an Existing Repository

The git clone command is used to create a local copy of a remote Git repository. This is useful when you want to contribute to an open-source project, work on a team project, or simply have a local copy of a repository for offline work.

To clone a remote repository:

1. Obtain the Repository's URL: You can usually find the repository's URL on the platform where it's hosted (e.g., GitHub, GitLab, Bitbucket). It typically looks like https://github.com/username/repository-name.git.
2. Run the git clone Command: Open your terminal and type the following command, replacing the URL with the actual repository URL:

Bash

```
git clone
https://github.com/username/repository-name.git
```

This command will create a new directory with the same name as the repository and populate it with all the files and history from the remote repository.

Key Points:

* Cloning a Specific Directory: You can clone a specific directory within a repository using the --depth option:

Bash

```
git clone --depth 1
https://github.com/username/repository-name.git
```

- This will clone only the latest commit history.
- Cloning a Bare Repository: To clone a bare repository (a repository without a working directory), use the --bare option:

Bash

```
git clone --bare
https://github.com/username/repository-name.git
```

- This creates a new repository without a working directory, often used for mirroring or archival purposes.

By using the git clone command, you can easily obtain and work on code from remote repositories.

3.3 git add: Staging Changes

Before you can commit changes to your Git repository, you need to stage them. The git add command is used to add changes to the staging area, which is like a temporary holding area for changes.

To stage changes:

1. Make Changes to Your Files: Edit your files as needed.
2. Stage Changes: Use the git add command to stage specific files or all changes in the current directory:

Bash

```
# Stage a specific file:

git add filename.txt
```

```
# Stage all changes in the current directory:

git add .
```

Understanding the Staging Area:

- Temporary Holding Area: The staging area is a temporary buffer where you can prepare changes for commit.
- Selective Commits: You can stage specific changes, allowing you to commit only the desired modifications.
- Reviewing Changes: The staging area provides an opportunity to review changes before committing them.

Key Points:

- Staging Multiple Files: You can stage multiple files by separating them with spaces:

Bash

```
git add file1.txt file2.py
```

- Unstaging Changes: If you want to unstage a file, use the git reset command:

Bash

```
git reset filename.txt
```

- Checking the Staging Area: Use the git status command to see which files are staged and which are not.

By effectively using the git add command, you can control the changes that are included in your commits, ensuring a clean and organized project history.

3.4 git commit: Committing Changes

Once you've staged your changes using git add, the next step is to commit them to your Git repository. A commit is a snapshot of your project at a specific point in time.

To commit changes:

1. Stage Changes: Ensure that you've staged the desired changes using the git add command.
2. Create a Commit: Use the git commit command to create a commit with a descriptive message:

Bash

```
git commit -m "Your commit message"
```

3. Replace "Your commit message" with a clear and concise message that explains the purpose of the changes.

Key Points:

- Descriptive Commit Messages: Write meaningful commit messages that clearly convey the changes made.
- Multiple Commits: You can create multiple commits for a single set of changes by staging and committing them in smaller chunks.
- Amending the Last Commit: If you need to add more changes to the last commit, use the --amend flag:

Bash

```
git commit --amend -m "Updated commit message"
```

Best Practices for Commit Messages:

- Clear and Concise: Keep your messages brief and to the point.
- Present Tense: Use the present tense to describe the changes.
- Start with a Verb: Begin your message with a verb like "Add," "Fix," or "Improve."
- Explain the Why: Briefly explain the reason for the changes.

By following these guidelines, you can create a well-organized and understandable commit history.

3.5 git status: Checking Repository Status

The git status command is a valuable tool for checking the current state of your Git repository. It provides information about:

- Untracked Files: Files that have been added to the directory but not yet tracked by Git.
- Changes Not Staged for Commit: Modified files that have not been staged for commit.
- Changes Staged for Commit: Files that are ready to be committed.
- Branch Information: The current branch and any local branches that have not been merged.

To check the status of your repository:

1. Open your terminal or command prompt.
2. Navigate to your Git repository directory.
3. Run the git status command:

Bash

```
git status
```

Example Output:

On branch main

Your branch is up to date with 'origin/main'.

Changes not staged for commit:

 (use "git add <file>..." to update what will be committed)

 (use[1] "git checkout -- <file>..." to discard changes in working
directory)

  modified: README.md

Changes to be committed:

 (use "git reset HEAD <file>..." to unstage)[2]

  modified: main.py

Interpreting the Output:

- Untracked Files: Listed under "Changes not staged for
  commit."
- Changes Not Staged: Modified files that are not ready for
  commit.
- Changes Staged for Commit: Files that are ready to be
  committed.

- Branch Information: Indicates the current branch and its status.

Using git status Effectively:

- Monitor Changes: Use git status to keep track of your progress and identify any potential conflicts.
- Plan Commits: Use the output to decide which changes to commit together.
- Identify Issues: Quickly spot untracked files or changes that might cause problems.
- Guide Your Workflow: Use git status to guide your development process and make informed decisions.

By regularly using git status, you can maintain a clear understanding of your repository's state and make informed decisions about your next steps.

3.6 git log: Viewing Commit History

The git log command allows you to view the history of commits in your Git repository. It provides valuable information about when changes were made, who made them, and what changes were included.

To view the commit history:

1. Open your terminal or command prompt.
2. Navigate to your Git repository directory.
3. Run the git log command:

Bash

```
git log
```

This will display a list of commits, each with a unique hash, author, date, and commit message.

Understanding the Output:

- Commit Hash: A unique identifier for each commit.
- Author: The person who made the commit.
- Date: The date and time the commit was made.
- Commit Message: A brief description of the changes made in the commit.

Customizing the git log Output:

You can customize the output of git log using various options:

- Viewing a Specific Number of Commits:

Bash

```
git log -n 5
```

- This will show the last 5 commits.
- Viewing Commits in a Specific Date Range:

Bash

```
git log --since="2 weeks ago" --until="1 week ago"
```

- This will show commits made between two specific dates.
- Viewing Commits by Author:

Bash

```
git log --author="Your Name"
```

- This will show commits made by a specific author.
- Viewing Commits in a Specific Format:

Bash

```
git log --pretty=format:"%h - %an, %ar: %s"
```

- This will display the commit hash, author name, relative date, and subject in a specific format.

By using the git log command, you can gain valuable insights into the development history of your project, identify specific changes, and learn from past mistakes.

3.7 git diff: Comparing Changes

The git diff command is a powerful tool for comparing changes between different versions of your code. It allows you to see exactly what has changed, making it easier to review and understand modifications.

To compare changes:

1. Open your terminal or command prompt.
2. Navigate to your Git repository directory.
3. Run the git diff command:

Bash

```
git diff
```

This command will show the differences between the current state of your working directory and the latest commit.

Understanding the Output:

The output of git diff is typically a side-by-side comparison of the original and modified code, highlighting the differences using color-coding.

Customizing the git diff Output:

You can customize the git diff output using various options:

- Comparing Specific Files:

Bash

```
git diff filename.txt
```

- This will compare the current version of filename.txt with the latest committed version.
- Comparing Different Commits:

Bash

```
git diff commit1 commit2
```

- This will compare the changes between two specific commits.
- Comparing Branches:

Bash

```
git diff branch1 branch2
```

- This will compare the differences between two branches.
- Viewing a Detailed Diff:

Bash

```
git diff --name-only
```

- This will list the files that have changed.

Bash

git diff --stat

- This will show a summary of the changes, including the number of files changed and lines added/deleted.

By using the git diff command effectively, you can identify and understand changes, review code, and debug issues more efficiently.

Part II

Branching and Merging

Chapter 4: Branching

4.1 Understanding Branches

A branch in Git is essentially a separate line of development. It allows you to work on a specific feature, bug fix, or experiment without affecting the main codebase. This is a powerful feature that enables parallel development and risk-free experimentation.

Why Use Branches?

- Isolated Development: Work on new features or bug fixes without affecting the main codebase.
- Experimentation: Try out new ideas without risking the stability of the main project.
- Collaboration: Multiple developers can work on different branches simultaneously.
- Feature Toggles: Enable or disable features based on specific conditions.

Types of Branches:

- Main Branch (often called main or master): The primary branch of your project.
- Feature Branches: Created for specific features or functionalities.
- Bugfix Branches: Created to fix specific bugs.
- Hotfix Branches: Created to quickly fix urgent issues in production.

Key Concepts:

- Branching: Creating a new branch from an existing one.
- Switching Branches: Moving between different branches.
- Merging Branches: Combining changes from one branch into another.

By understanding branches, you can effectively organize your development work, collaborate with others, and manage complex projects.

4.2 Creating a New Branch

To create a new branch in Git, you use the git branch command. This command allows you to create a new branch from the current one, giving you a separate line of development to work on.

To create a new branch:

1. Open your terminal or command prompt.
2. Navigate to your Git repository directory.
3. Run the git branch <branch-name> command:

Bash

```
git branch feature-branch
```

4. This will create a new branch named feature-branch.

Switching to the New Branch:

To start working on the newly created branch, you need to switch to it using the git checkout command:

Bash

```
git checkout feature-branch
```

Creating a Branch and Switching to It Simultaneously:

You can combine the creation and switching steps into a single command:

Bash

```bash
git checkout -b feature-branch
```

Key Points:

- Branch Naming: Use descriptive names for your branches to easily identify their purpose.
- Multiple Branches: You can create multiple branches to work on different features or bug fixes simultaneously.
- Branching Strategy: Consider using a branching strategy like Gitflow to organize your workflow effectively.

By creating branches, you can isolate your work, experiment with new ideas, and collaborate with others without affecting the main codebase.

4.3 Switching Between Branches

Once you've created multiple branches, you can easily switch between them using the git checkout command. This allows you to work on different parts of your project without affecting each other.

To switch to a specific branch:

1. Open your terminal or command prompt.
2. Navigate to your Git repository directory.
3. Run the git checkout <branch-name> command:

Bash

```bash
git checkout feature-branch
```

4. This will switch your working directory to the feature-branch branch.

Key Points:

- Checking the Current Branch: To see which branch you're currently on, use the git branch command without any arguments.

Bash

```
git branch
```

- The branch you're currently on will be marked with an asterisk (*).
- Creating and Switching in One Step: You can create a new branch and switch to it in a single step:

Bash

```
git checkout -b new-branch-name
```

-
-
- Discarding Changes: If you've made changes to the current branch that you don't want to keep, you can discard them using the --force option with checkout:

Bash

```
git checkout --force main
```

Caution: Use this option with caution, as it will discard any uncommitted changes.

By effectively switching between branches, you can manage your development workflow, isolate features, and collaborate with others seamlessly.

4.4 Viewing Branches

To get a list of all branches in your Git repository, you can use the git branch command. This command provides information about the current branch and all other local branches.

To view the list of branches:

1. Open your terminal or command prompt.
2. Navigate to your Git repository directory.
3. Run the git branch command:

Bash

```
git branch
```

This will output a list of branches, with the current branch marked with an asterisk (*).

Example Output:

```
* main

  feature-branch

  bugfix-branch
```

Understanding the Output:

- Current Branch: The branch marked with an asterisk is the currently active branch.
- Other Branches: The remaining branches listed are other local branches in your repository.

Additional Tips:

- Viewing Remote Branches: To view remote branches, use the -r flag:

Bash

```
git branch -r
```

- Viewing All Branches (Local and Remote):

Bash

```
git branch -a
```

- Viewing Detailed Branch Information:

Bash

```
git branch -v
```

- This will show the latest commit hash and message for each branch.

By using the git branch command, you can easily keep track of your branches and understand the overall structure of your Git repository.

4.5 Deleting Branches

Once you've finished working on a branch and no longer need it, you can delete it to keep your repository clean and organized.

To delete a branch:

1. Open your terminal or command prompt.
2. Navigate to your Git repository directory.
3. Run the git branch -d <branch-name> command:

Bash

```
git branch -d feature-branch
```

4. This will delete the feature-branch branch.

Important Considerations:

- Merged Branches: If a branch has been merged into another branch, you can safely delete it.
- Unmerged Branches: Be cautious when deleting unmerged branches, as you may lose important changes.
- Remote Branches: To delete a remote branch, you'll need to use a command like git push origin --delete <branch-name>.

Best Practices:

- Clean Up Regularly: Delete unnecessary branches to keep your repository organized.
- Review Before Deleting: Double-check that you've merged or discarded any important changes before deleting a branch.
- Use a Branching Strategy: A well-defined branching strategy can help you manage your branches effectively.

By following these guidelines, you can maintain a clean and efficient Git repository.

Chapter 5: Merging

5.1 Merging Branches

Merging is the process of combining changes from one branch into another. This is typically done when you've finished working on a feature or bug fix and want to integrate the changes into the main branch.

To merge a branch:

1. Checkout the Target Branch: Switch to the branch you want to merge into (usually the main branch).

Bash

```
git checkout main
```

2. Merge the Source Branch: Use the git merge command to merge the source branch into the current branch:

Bash

```
git merge feature-branch
```

3. This will merge the changes from the feature-branch into the main branch.

Types of Merges:

- Fast-Forward Merge: If the target branch is a direct ancestor of the source branch, Git can perform a fast-forward merge, simply moving the target branch's pointer to the latest commit of the source branch.

- Merge Commit: If the branches have diverged, Git creates a new merge commit that combines the changes from both branches.

Resolving Merge Conflicts:

If there are conflicts between the changes in the two branches, Git will stop the merge process and prompt you to resolve the conflicts manually. You can use a merge tool or edit the files directly to resolve the conflicts. Once the conflicts are resolved, you can stage the resolved files and commit the merge.

Best Practices:

- Frequent Merging: Merge your branches regularly to avoid large and complex merge conflicts.
- Small, Focused Commits: Make small, focused commits to simplify the merge process.
- Use a Merge Tool: A merge tool can help you visualize and resolve conflicts more easily.
- Test Thoroughly: After merging, thoroughly test your code to ensure that the changes have been integrated correctly.

By understanding the merging process and following best practices, you can effectively combine changes from different branches and maintain a clean and organized Git history.

5.2 Resolving Merge Conflicts

When merging branches, conflicts can arise if both branches have made changes to the same part of a file. Git will indicate these conflicts and pause the merge process.

Identifying Merge Conflicts:

- Conflict Markers: Git will add special markers to the conflicting files, indicating the conflicting sections.

- Error Messages: Git will display error messages indicating the files with conflicts.

Resolving Merge Conflicts:

1. Manual Resolution:
   - Open the conflicting files in a text editor.
   - Identify the conflicting sections, which will be marked with special markers.
   - Decide which changes to keep and which to discard.
   - Manually edit the files to resolve the conflicts.
2. Using a Merge Tool:
   - Many Git clients and IDEs have built-in merge tools that can help you visualize and resolve conflicts.
   - These tools often provide a graphical interface to compare changes and choose the desired outcome.

Resolving Conflicts in the Command Line:

1. Stage the Resolved Files: Once you've resolved the conflicts, stage the files:

Bash

```
git add filename.txt
```

2. Commit the Merge: Commit the merge with a descriptive message:

Bash

```
git commit -m "Merged feature-branch with conflict resolution"
```

Preventing Merge Conflicts:

- Frequent Merging: Merge your branches regularly to minimize the risk of large conflicts.
- Small, Focused Commits: Make smaller, more focused commits to reduce the likelihood of conflicts.
- Clear Communication: Communicate with your team members to coordinate work and avoid overlapping changes.
- Use a Branching Strategy: A well-defined branching strategy can help you manage your branches effectively and reduce the risk of conflicts.

By understanding the process of resolving merge conflicts and following best practices, you can efficiently manage conflicts and maintain a clean Git history.

5.3 Strategies for Merging: Fast-Forward vs. Merge Commit

When merging branches in Git, there are two primary strategies: fast-forward merge and merge commit. The choice between these strategies depends on the relationship between the branches.

Fast-Forward Merge

A fast-forward merge is the simplest type of merge. It occurs when the target branch is a direct ancestor of the source branch. In other words, the target branch has all the commits that the source branch has, plus possibly more.

How it works:

1. Identify the Common Ancestor: Git determines the latest common commit between the two branches.
2. Move the Target Branch: Git simply moves the target branch's pointer to the latest commit of the source branch.

Advantages of Fast-Forward Merges:

- Clean History: The commit history remains linear, without unnecessary merge commits.
- Efficient: It's a faster and simpler operation.

Merge Commit

A merge commit is created when the two branches have diverged, meaning they have commits that are not shared between them. In this case, Git creates a new commit that combines the changes from both branches.

How it works:

1. Identify the Merge Base: Git determines the latest common ancestor of the two branches.
2. Create a Merge Commit: Git creates a new commit that merges the changes from both branches. This new commit has two parent commits: the latest commit from each branch.

Advantages of Merge Commits:

- Preserves History: A merge commit records the point where two branches diverged and merged.
- Clearer History: It can help visualize the branching and merging history of a project.

Choosing the Right Strategy:

- Fast-Forward Merges:
    - Use when the target branch is a direct ancestor of the source branch.
    - Ideal for simple, linear development workflows.
- Merge Commits:
    - Use when the branches have diverged and have unique commits.
    - Provides a clear record of the merge point.

By understanding these two strategies, you can make informed decisions about how to merge branches in your Git workflow.

Part III

Remote Repositories

Chapter 6: Remote Repositories

6.1 Understanding Remote Repositories

A remote repository is a version-controlled project that is hosted on a remote server. It allows you to collaborate with other developers, share your code, and back up your work.

Why Use Remote Repositories?

- Collaboration: Multiple developers can work on the same project simultaneously.
- Backup: Your code is backed up on a remote server, protecting it from accidental loss.
- Sharing: You can share your code with the world and collaborate on open-source projects.
- Version Control: Remote repositories provide a central location for managing your project's history.

Popular Remote Repository Hosting Services:

- GitHub: A popular platform for hosting public and private repositories.
- GitLab: A comprehensive platform for software development, including version control, issue tracking, and CI/CD.
- Bitbucket: A platform for professional teams, offering private repositories and advanced features.

Key Concepts:

- Origin: The default name for the remote repository that you clone from.
- Remote Tracking Branches: Local branches that track the state of remote branches.

- Pushing and Pulling: Actions to transfer changes between local and remote repositories.

By understanding remote repositories, you can effectively collaborate with others, share your code, and leverage the benefits of distributed version control.

6.2 Adding a Remote Repository

To collaborate with others or back up your code, you'll need to add a remote repository to your local Git repository. This remote repository is typically hosted on a platform like GitHub, GitLab, or Bitbucket.

To add a remote repository:

1. Obtain the Remote Repository's URL: Get the URL of the remote repository you want to add. This is usually a HTTPS or SSH URL.
2. Use the git remote add Command: Open your terminal and navigate to your local repository directory. Then, run the following command, replacing origin with a name for the remote and the URL with the actual remote repository URL:

Bash

```
git remote add origin
https://github.com/username/repository-name.git
```

3. You can use any name for the remote, but origin is a common convention.

Verifying the Remote Repository:

To verify that the remote repository has been added, you can use the git remote -v command:

Bash

```
git remote -v
```

This will display a list of your remote repositories, along with their URLs for fetching and pushing.

Key Points:

- Multiple Remotes: You can add multiple remote repositories to your local repository.
- Renaming Remotes: You can rename a remote using the git remote rename command.
- Removing Remotes: You can remove a remote using the git remote remove command.

By adding remote repositories, you can collaborate with others, share your code, and keep your projects backed up.

6.3 Fetching and Pulling Changes

Once you've added a remote repository, you can fetch and pull changes from it to your local repository.

Fetching Changes

Fetching downloads the latest changes from the remote repository to your local repository without merging them into your current branch. This allows you to review the changes before integrating them.

To fetch changes:

1. Open your terminal or command prompt.
2. Navigate to your local repository directory.
3. Run the git fetch command:

4. Bash

git fetch origin

5. This command fetches the latest changes from the remote repository named origin.

Pulling Changes

Pulling combines fetching and merging changes from the remote repository into your current branch. This is useful when you want to update your local branch with the latest changes from the remote repository.

To pull changes:

1. Open your terminal or command prompt.
2. Navigate to your local repository directory.
3. Run the git pull command:

Bash

git pull origin main

4. This command fetches changes from the main branch of the remote repository origin and merges them into your current local branch.

Key Points:

- Fetching vs. Pulling:
  - Fetching: Downloads changes without merging.
  - Pulling: Fetches changes and merges them into the current branch.

- Resolving Conflicts: If there are conflicts between the local and remote changes, you'll need to resolve them manually.
- Specifying Remote and Branch: You can specify the remote and branch to fetch or pull from using the following syntax:

Bash

```
git fetch origin feature-branch
```

```
git pull origin feature-branch
```

By understanding the difference between fetching and pulling, you can effectively keep your local repository up-to-date with the latest changes from the remote repository.

6.4 Pushing Changes to a Remote Repository

Once you've made changes to your local repository, you can push those changes to a remote repository. This allows you to share your work with others and back up your code.

To push changes to a remote repository:

1. Stage and Commit Changes:

   Ensure that you've staged and committed your changes locally.

2. Push Changes to the Remote Repository:

Use the `git push` command to push your local branch to the remote repository:

```bash
git push origin main
```

This command pushes your local `main` branch to the remote `origin` repository's `main` branch.

Key Points:

Specifying Remote and Branch:

You can specify the remote and branch to push to:

```bash
git push origin feature-branch
```

This pushes your local `feature-branch` to the remote `origin` repository's `feature-branch`.

Setting Up SSH Keys:

To push changes to private repositories, you'll need to set up SSH keys to authenticate yourself.

Force Pushing:

Use with caution: You can force push changes to a remote branch using the `-f` flag:

```bash
git push -f origin main
```

This can overwrite the remote branch's history, so use it only when necessary.

By understanding how to push changes to a remote repository, you can effectively collaborate with others and share your work with the world.

Part IV

Advanced Git

Chapter 7: Git Workflows

7.1 Centralized Workflow

The centralized workflow is a simple and straightforward approach to version control, where a single, central repository acts as the primary source of truth. All developers work on a shared main branch and merge their changes directly into it.

How it works:

1. Single Repository: A central, shared repository is maintained.
2. Cloning the Repository: Developers clone this central repository to their local machines.
3. Making Changes: Developers make changes to their local copies.
4. Committing Changes: Changes are committed locally.
5. Pushing Changes: Commits are pushed to the central repository.
6. Pulling Changes: Developers periodically pull the latest changes from the central repository to their local machines.

Advantages of Centralized Workflow:

- Simplicity: Easy to understand and implement.
- Centralized Control: A single source of truth for the project.

Disadvantages of Centralized Workflow:

- Single Point of Failure: If the central server goes down, development is halted.
- Limited Offline Work: Developers may have difficulty working offline.
- Potential for Merge Conflicts: Frequent merging can lead to merge conflicts.

Best Practices for Centralized Workflow:

- Frequent Commits: Commit changes frequently to avoid large merge conflicts.
- Clear Communication: Communicate with other developers to coordinate work and avoid conflicts.
- Use a Good Merge Tool: A merge tool can help resolve conflicts efficiently.
- Consider a Distributed Workflow: For larger projects or distributed teams, a distributed workflow might be more suitable.

While the centralized workflow is simple to implement, it's important to be aware of its limitations and consider alternative workflows, such as the feature branch workflow, for more complex projects.

7.2 Feature Branch Workflow

The feature branch workflow is a popular Git workflow that promotes efficient and organized development. It involves creating separate branches for each new feature or bug fix, isolating development and minimizing the risk of introducing bugs into the main codebase.

How it works:

1. Create a Feature Branch: Create a new branch for each feature or bug fix:

Bash

```
git checkout -b feature-name
```

2. Develop the Feature: Work on the feature on the new branch.
3. Commit Changes: Commit changes to the feature branch.

4. Merge the Feature Branch: Once the feature is complete, merge the feature branch into the main branch:

Bash

```
git checkout main

git merge feature-name
```

5. Delete the Feature Branch: After merging, delete the feature branch to keep your repository clean:

Bash

```
git branch -d feature-name
```

Advantages of Feature Branch Workflow:

- Isolated Development: Developers can work on different features independently.
- Reduced Risk: Changes to the main codebase are controlled and less likely to introduce bugs.
- Easier Code Review: Feature branches can be reviewed and tested before merging.
- Flexible Workflows: Supports various development methodologies, such as Agile.

Best Practices for Feature Branch Workflow:

- Clear Branch Naming: Use descriptive names for branches to easily identify their purpose.
- Frequent Merging: Merge feature branches into the main branch regularly to avoid large merge conflicts.
- Code Review: Use a code review process to ensure code quality and consistency.

- Clean Up Branches: Delete merged branches to keep your repository organized.

By following the feature branch workflow, you can efficiently manage your development process, reduce the risk of errors, and improve code quality.

7.3 Forking Workflow

The forking workflow is a popular approach for open-source projects, allowing developers to contribute to projects without directly modifying the main repository. It involves creating a personal copy of the repository, making changes to the copy, and then submitting a pull request to the original repository.

How it works:

1. Fork the Repository: Create a personal copy of the original repository on a platform like GitHub. This creates a fork of the original repository.
2. Clone the Fork: Clone your forked repository to your local machine.
3. Create a Feature Branch: Create a new branch for your feature or bug fix.
4. Make Changes: Work on your feature or bug fix on the new branch.
5. Commit Changes: Commit your changes to the feature branch.
6. Push Changes to Your Fork: Push your feature branch to your forked repository.
7. Create a Pull Request: Submit a pull request to the original repository, requesting that your changes be merged into the main repository.
8. Review and Merge: The original repository's maintainers will review your pull request and merge it if approved.

Advantages of Forking Workflow:

- Decentralized Development: Developers can contribute to projects without direct access to the main repository.
- Reduced Risk: Changes to the main repository are controlled by the project maintainers.
- Community-Driven Development: Encourages community involvement and collaboration.
- Experimentation: Developers can experiment with new features or ideas without affecting the main project.

Best Practices for Forking Workflow:

- Follow Guidelines: Adhere to the project's coding standards and contribution guidelines.
- Write Clear Commit Messages: Use clear and concise commit messages to explain your changes.
- Respond to Feedback: Be open to feedback and make necessary changes to your pull request.
- Stay Up-to-Date: Regularly update your fork with the latest changes from the original repository.

By following the forking workflow, you can effectively contribute to open-source projects and collaborate with other developers.

7.4 Gitflow Workflow

Gitflow is a robust branching strategy that provides a structured approach to managing different stages of development, such as development, testing, and production. It involves a set of specific branches for various purposes.

Key Branches in Gitflow:

- Main Branch: The primary branch for production-ready code.
- Develop Branch: The main development branch where features are developed.
- Feature Branches: Short-lived branches created from the develop branch to implement specific features.

- Release Branches: Created from the develop branch to prepare for a release.
- Hotfix Branches: Created from the main branch to fix urgent bugs in production.

Workflow:

1. Feature Development:
    - Create a feature branch from the develop branch.
    - Develop the feature on the feature branch.
    - Commit changes to the feature branch.
2. Feature Integration:
    - Merge the feature branch into the develop branch.
    - Delete the feature branch.
3. Release Preparation:
    - Create a release branch from the develop branch.
    - Make any necessary fixes or changes to the release branch.
4. Release:
    - Merge the release branch into the main branch.
    - Tag the release commit.
    - Deploy the release to production.
5. Hotfix:
    - Create a hotfix branch from the main branch.
    - Fix the bug on the hotfix branch.
    - Merge the hotfix branch into both the main and develop branches.
    - Delete the hotfix branch.

Advantages of Gitflow:

- Clear Structure: Provides a well-defined structure for managing different stages of development.
- Stable Main Branch: Ensures the stability of the production branch.
- Efficient Releases: Streamlines the release process.

- Flexible for Complex Projects: Suitable for large-scale projects with multiple teams.

Disadvantages of Gitflow:

- Complexity: Can be complex for small projects or teams.
- Steep Learning Curve: Requires a good understanding of Git concepts.
- Overhead: Can add overhead to the development process, especially for smaller projects.

While Gitflow is a powerful workflow, it's important to choose a workflow that best suits your team's needs and project complexity. For smaller projects, a simpler workflow like feature branching might be sufficient.

Chapter 8: Git History Manipulation

8.1 Resetting the HEAD Pointer

The HEAD pointer in Git refers to the currently checked-out commit. Resetting the HEAD pointer allows you to move it to a different commit, effectively changing the current state of your working directory.

Types of Resets:

1. Soft Reset:
    - Moves the HEAD pointer to a previous commit without changing the staging area.
    - Unstaged changes are preserved.
    - Use case: Undoing recent commits without losing changes.
2. Mixed Reset:
    - Moves the HEAD pointer to a previous commit and resets the staging area to match that commit.
    - Unstaged changes are lost.
    - Use case: Undoing part of a commit or resetting a branch to a specific point.
3. Hard Reset:
    - Moves the HEAD pointer to a previous commit and resets the staging area and working directory to match that commit.
    - All uncommitted changes are lost.
    - Use case: Discarding unwanted changes or reverting to a previous state.

How to Reset the HEAD Pointer:

To reset the HEAD pointer, use the git reset command with the appropriate mode:

Soft Reset:

Bash

git reset --soft HEAD~1

This moves the HEAD pointer to the previous commit, preserving unstaged changes.

Mixed Reset:

Bash

git reset --mixed HEAD~1

This moves the HEAD pointer and resets the staging area to the previous commit.

Hard Reset:

Bash

git reset --hard HEAD~1

This moves the HEAD pointer, resets the staging area, and discards uncommitted changes.

Caution:

- Hard Resets are irreversible: Use them with caution, as they permanently delete uncommitted changes.

- Remote Repositories: Resetting the HEAD pointer locally does not affect remote repositories. You'll need to push the changes to the remote repository to share them.

By understanding the different types of resets and their implications, you can effectively manipulate your Git history and recover from mistakes.

8.2 Reversing Commits

Sometimes, you might need to undo a commit that you've made. Git provides several ways to reverse commits, depending on the specific situation.

Using git revert

The git revert command creates a new commit that undoes the changes introduced by a specific commit. This is a safe way to reverse commits without affecting the original commit history.

To reverse a commit:

1. Identify the Commit Hash: Use git log to find the hash of the commit you want to reverse.
2. Revert the Commit:

Bash

```
git revert <commit-hash>
```

This will create a new commit that undoes the changes introduced by the specified commit.

Using git reset

The git reset command can also be used to undo commits, but it's important to use it carefully, as it can modify the commit history.

Soft Reset: This moves the HEAD pointer to a previous commit without changing the staging area. You can use this to undo a commit and keep the changes staged for a new commit.

Mixed Reset: This moves the HEAD pointer to a previous commit and resets the staging area. Any unstaged changes will be lost.

Hard Reset: This moves the HEAD pointer to a previous commit and resets the staging area and working directory. All uncommitted changes will be lost.

Caution:

- Hard Resets are irreversible: Use them with caution, as they permanently delete uncommitted changes.
- Remote Repositories: Reversing commits locally does not affect remote repositories. You'll need to push the changes to the remote repository to share them.

By understanding these methods, you can effectively reverse commits and recover from mistakes.

8.3 Interactive Rebase

Interactive rebase is a powerful tool that allows you to modify the commit history of a branch. It gives you fine-grained control over your commits, enabling you to reorder, squash, edit, or remove them.

How to Use Interactive Rebase:

Start the Interactive Rebase:

Bash

```
git rebase -i HEAD~<number-of-commits>
```

1. Replace <number-of-commits> with the number of commits you want to rebase. This will open your default text editor with a list of commits.
2. Edit the Commit List: You can edit the list of commits using the following commands:
   - pick: Keep the commit as is.
   - reword: Revise the commit message.
   - edit: Stop the rebase process and allow you to edit the commit.
   - squash: Combine the commit with the previous one.
   - fixup: Combine the commit with the previous one, discarding the commit message.
   - drop: Discard the commit entirely.
3. Save and Exit: Save the edited file and exit the text editor. Git will perform the rebase operations based on your instructions.

Key Points:

- Reordering Commits: You can reorder commits by changing their order in the list.
- Squashing Commits: You can combine multiple small commits into a single commit.
- Editing Commit Messages: You can modify the commit messages of individual commits.
- Discarding Commits: You can remove unwanted commits from the history.

Caution:

- Use with Care: Interactive rebase can significantly modify the commit history, so use it with caution.
- Remote Repositories: If you've pushed your branch to a remote repository, be careful when using interactive rebase, as it can create conflicts when you push the changes.

Best Practices:

- Use Descriptive Commit Messages: Clear commit messages make it easier to understand the changes made.
- Rebase Frequently: Rebase your feature branches regularly to keep your commit history clean and linear.
- Test Thoroughly: After rebasing, test your code to ensure that it still works as expected.

By mastering interactive rebase, you can create a clean and well-structured commit history, making it easier to collaborate with others and maintain your codebase.

8.4 Cherry-Picking Commits

Cherry-picking allows you to select specific commits from one branch and apply them to another. This is useful when you want to apply a particular change from one branch to another without merging the entire branch.

How to Cherry-Pick a Commit:

1. Identify the Commit Hash: Use git log to find the hash of the commit you want to cherry-pick.
2. Cherry-Pick the Commit: Use the git cherry-pick command:

Bash

```
git cherry-pick <commit-hash>
```

3. This will apply the changes from the specified commit to your current branch.

Key Points:

- Resolving Conflicts: If there are conflicts between the cherry-picked commit and the current branch, you'll need to resolve them manually.

- Multiple Commits: You can cherry-pick multiple commits by specifying their hashes one by one.
- Cherry-Picking from Remote Branches: You can cherry-pick commits from remote branches by specifying the remote and branch name:

Bash

```
git cherry-pick origin/feature-branch/<commit-hash>
```

Use Cases for Cherry-Picking:

- Applying a Bug Fix: Cherry-pick a bug fix from a hotfix branch to the main branch.
- Reusing a Feature: Cherry-pick a feature from one branch to another.
- Experimenting with Changes: Cherry-pick a specific change to test it in a different context.

Caution:

- Carefully Consider the Impact: Cherry-picking can sometimes lead to unexpected results, especially if the cherry-picked commit has dependencies on other commits.
- Test Thoroughly: After cherry-picking a commit, it's important to test your code to ensure that the changes have been applied correctly.

By understanding cherry-picking, you can selectively apply changes from one branch to another, providing flexibility and control over your development workflow.

Chapter 9: Git Tools and Tips

9.1 Git Aliases

Git aliases allow you to create shortcuts for frequently used Git commands. This can significantly improve your efficiency and make your Git workflow more streamlined.

Creating a Git Alias:

To create a Git alias, use the git config command:

Bash

```
git config --global alias.<alias-name> <command>
```

Replace <alias-name> with the desired alias name and <command> with the actual Git command.

Example:

To create an alias for the git status command, you would use:

Bash

```
git config --global alias.st status
```

Now, you can use the git st command to check the status of your repository.

Common Git Aliases:

Here are some common Git aliases that you might find useful:

- co: git checkout
- ci: git commit
- br: git branch
- log: git log --oneline --graph --decorate
- diff: git diff --name-status
- push: git push origin
- pull: git pull origin

Customizing Your Git Workflow:

You can create custom aliases to suit your specific needs. For example, you could create an alias to commit and push changes in one step:

Bash

```bash
git config --global alias.cp 'commit -m "Commit message" && push'
```

Using Aliases in Scripts:

You can also use Git aliases in scripts to automate common tasks. For example, you could create a script to automatically create a new branch, switch to it, and make an initial commit:

Bash

```bash
#!/bin/bash

git checkout -b new-feature

git commit -m "Initial commit for new feature"
```

By creating and using Git aliases, you can significantly improve your Git workflow and make your daily tasks more efficient.

9.2 Git Configuration

Git configuration allows you to customize various aspects of your Git environment, such as your username, email address, default editor, and more. This customization can significantly improve your workflow and make Git more efficient.

Global Configuration:

Global configuration settings apply to all Git repositories on your system. To set global configuration options, use the --global flag:

Bash

```
git config --global user.name "Your Name"

git config --global user.email "your_email@example.com"

git config --global core.editor[1] "vim"
```

Local Configuration:

Local configuration settings apply only to the specific repository you're currently in. To set local configuration options, omit the --global flag:

Bash

```
git config user.name "Your Name (Project-Specific)"

git config user.email "your_email@example.com (Project-Specific)"
```

Checking Configuration:

To view your current Git configuration, use the git config --list command:

Bash

```
git config --list
```

Editing the Configuration File Directly:

You can also edit your Git configuration file directly. The default location for this file is:

- Windows: C:\Users\YourUserName\.gitconfig
- macOS/Linux: ~/.gitconfig

Common Configuration Options:

- user.name and user.email: Set your name and email address for commit authorship.
- core.editor: Set your preferred text editor for commit messages and other interactive operations.
- core.autocrlf: Configure how Git handles line endings.
- push.default: Set the default behavior for the git push command.
- merge.tool: Set a default merge tool for resolving conflicts.

Additional Tips:

- Use Git Aliases: Create aliases for frequently used Git commands to save time.
- Consider a Git GUI: A Git GUI can simplify complex operations and provide a visual interface.

- Experiment with Different Configurations: Try different configurations to find what works best for you.

By understanding Git configuration, you can tailor your Git environment to your specific needs and preferences, making your development workflow more efficient and enjoyable.

9.3 Git Hooks

Git hooks are scripts that automatically run at specific points in the Git workflow. They allow you to customize your Git experience and automate various tasks. Git hooks can be used to:

- Validate code: Ensure code quality and consistency.
- Format code: Automatically format code according to specific style guidelines.
- Send notifications: Notify team members about code changes or deployments.
- Run tests: Automatically run tests before committing or pushing code.

Types of Git Hooks:

There are two main types of Git hooks:

1. Client-Side Hooks: These hooks run on the local machine and are triggered by actions like committing, pushing, or receiving updates.
2. Server-Side Hooks: These hooks run on the server and are triggered by actions like receiving pushes or creating new branches.

Common Client-Side Hooks:

- pre-commit: Runs before a commit is made. It can be used to check code formatting, run tests, or prevent commits with certain patterns.

- post-commit: Runs after a commit is made. It can be used to send notifications, update issue trackers, or trigger other actions.
- pre-push: Runs before code is pushed to a remote repository. It can be used to validate the code, run tests, or prevent pushes with certain conditions.
- post-push: Runs after code is pushed to a remote repository. It can be used to deploy the code, send notifications, or trigger other actions.

Creating Git Hooks:

1. Navigate to the .git/hooks directory:

Bash

```
cd .git/hooks
```

2. Create a Hook Script: Create a script file with the same name as the hook you want to create (e.g., pre-commit).
3. Write the Script: Write the script in a language like Bash, Python, or Ruby. The script can perform various tasks, such as checking code formatting, running tests, or sending notifications.
4. Make the Script Executable: Make the script executable by running the following command:

Bash

```
chmod +x pre-commit
```

Example: A Simple Pre-commit Hook to Check for a Commit Message:

Bash

```bash
#!/bin/bash

# Check if a commit message is provided

if [ -z "$GIT_COMMIT_MESSAGE" ]; then

  echo "Please enter a commit message."

  exit 1

fi
```

By effectively using Git hooks, you can automate tasks, improve code quality, and streamline your development workflow.

9.4 Git Submodules

Git submodules allow you to include another Git repository as a subdirectory within your main repository. This is useful when you want to manage a specific part of your project separately or include third-party libraries.

How to Use Git Submodules:

Initialize a Submodule:

Bash

```bash
git submodule add
https://github.com/user/submodule.git submodule-dir
```

1. This command adds the specified remote repository as a submodule and places it in the submodule-dir directory.

2. Clone a Repository with Submodules: To clone a repository with submodules, use the --recursive flag:

Bash

```
git clone --recursive
https://github.com/user/main-repository.git
```

3. Initialize Submodules: After cloning a repository with submodules, you need to initialize them:

Bash

```
git submodule init

git submodule update --init --recursive
```

Working with Submodules:

- Updating Submodules: To update a submodule to the latest version, use the git submodule update command:

Bash

```
git submodule update --remote --merge submodule-dir
```

- Making Changes to a Submodule: To make changes to a submodule, navigate to the submodule directory and commit and push changes as usual.
- Adding a New Submodule: Use the git submodule add command to add a new submodule.

Key Points:

- Submodule Structure: Submodules are stored as a reference to the remote repository, not a full copy of the code.
- Submodule Updates: You need to manually update submodules to get the latest changes.
- Complex Workflows: Submodules can make your workflow more complex, especially when working with many submodules.

Alternatives to Submodules:

While submodules can be useful in certain situations, there are alternative approaches that may be more suitable for some projects:

- Subtrees: Subtrees allow you to integrate a subproject's code directly into your main repository.
- External Dependencies: If you need to include third-party libraries, consider using package managers like npm, pip, or Maven.

By understanding the concepts and limitations of Git submodules, you can make informed decisions about when and how to use them in your projects.

9.5 Git Large File Storage (LFS)

Git is primarily designed to handle text-based files efficiently. However, when working with large binary files such as images, videos, or large datasets, Git can become slow and inefficient. Git Large File Storage (LFS) is a solution to this problem. It allows you to store large files outside of the Git repository, while still tracking them in Git.

How Git LFS Works:

1. Installation: Install the Git LFS command-line tool.
2. Track Large Files: Configure Git LFS to track specific file extensions (e.g., .png, .jpg, .mp4).

3. Commit Changes: When you commit changes, Git LFS replaces large files with pointers to the LFS server.
4. Clone the Repository: When you clone a repository with LFS, Git LFS automatically downloads the large files.

Advantages of Git LFS:

- Improved Performance: Faster cloning, fetching, and pushing.
- Reduced Repository Size: Smaller Git repositories.
- Efficient Handling of Large Files: Optimized storage and transfer of large files.
- Seamless Integration: Integrates seamlessly with Git workflows.

Key Points:

- Configuration: Configure Git LFS to track specific file extensions or patterns.
- Storage Limits: LFS often has storage limits, so be mindful of your usage.
- Additional Setup: You may need to set up an LFS server or use a hosted LFS service.
- Potential Costs: Some LFS services may have associated costs, especially for large-scale projects.

By using Git LFS, you can effectively manage large files in your Git repositories, improving performance and collaboration.

Part V

Collaborative Development with Git

Chapter 10: Collaborative Development

10.1 Setting Up a Shared Repository

To collaborate effectively on a Git project, you'll need to set up a shared repository where multiple developers can work together. Here's a step-by-step guide on how to set up a shared repository:

1. Choose a Hosting Platform

- GitHub: A popular platform for both public and private repositories.
- GitLab: A comprehensive platform offering various features like issue tracking, CI/CD pipelines, and more.
- Bitbucket: A platform focused on professional teams, offering private repositories and advanced features.

2. Create a New Repository

- Sign Up: Create an account on your chosen platform.
- Create a New Repository: Follow the platform's instructions to create a new repository.
- Choose Repository Settings: Select appropriate settings like visibility (public or private), access permissions, and collaboration features.

3. Add a Remote Repository

- Clone the Repository: Clone the newly created repository to your local machine:

Bash

```
git clone
https://github.com/your-username/your-repository.git
```

- Add a Remote: If you already have a local repository, add the remote repository:

Bash

```
git remote add origin
https://github.com/your-username/your-repository.git
```

4. Collaborate with Others

- Grant Access: Invite other team members to collaborate on the repository.
- Create Branches: Each team member can create their own feature branches.
- Commit Changes: Commit changes to their local branches.
- Push Changes: Push changes to their remote branches.
- Create Pull Requests: Create pull requests to merge changes into the main branch.
- Review and Merge: Review pull requests, provide feedback, and merge approved changes.

Best Practices:

- Clear Communication: Use a communication tool like Slack, Teams, or a project management tool to discuss project requirements and coordinate work.
- Frequent Commits: Commit changes frequently and write clear commit messages.
- Regularly Push Changes: Push changes to the remote repository regularly to keep it up-to-date.

- Use a Branching Strategy: A well-defined branching strategy can help organize your workflow and reduce conflicts.
- Code Review: Implement a code review process to ensure code quality and consistency.

By following these steps and best practices, you can effectively set up a shared Git repository and collaborate with your team to build high-quality software.

10.2 Collaborating with Others

Effective collaboration is essential for successful software development. Git provides several tools and strategies to facilitate teamwork:

1. Forking and Pull Requests:

- Forking: Create a personal copy of the main repository.
- Branching: Create a new branch for your feature or bug fix.
- Committing Changes: Commit your changes to the branch.
- Pushing Changes: Push your branch to your forked repository.
- Creating a Pull Request: Submit a pull request to the main repository, requesting that your changes be merged.

2. Code Review:

- Reviewing Changes: Carefully review the code in pull requests.
- Providing Feedback: Offer constructive feedback and suggestions for improvement.
- Discussing Changes: Use the comment and discussion features of your platform to discuss changes.
- Merging Changes: Merge approved pull requests into the main branch.

3. Resolving Merge Conflicts:

- Identify Conflicts: Git will highlight conflicting changes in the merge process.
- Resolve Conflicts: Manually edit the files to resolve conflicts.
- Stage Resolved Files: Stage the resolved files using git add.
- Commit the Merge: Commit the merged changes.

4. Using a Shared Repository:

- Centralized Repository: All team members work on a single shared repository.
- Branching Strategy: Use a well-defined branching strategy to organize work.
- Direct Pushing: Developers can directly push their changes to the shared repository.
- Code Review: Use a code review process to ensure quality.

Best Practices for Collaboration:

- Clear Communication: Use effective communication channels to discuss project requirements, timelines, and technical issues.
- Regular Commits: Commit changes frequently and write clear commit messages.
- Test Thoroughly: Test your code before pushing changes to the remote repository.
- Respectful Collaboration: Be respectful and open to feedback from your team members.
- Use a Good Git Workflow: Choose a workflow that suits your team's needs and project complexity.

By following these guidelines and leveraging Git's powerful collaboration features, you can work effectively with your team to build high-quality software.

10.3 Resolving Merge Conflicts

When multiple developers work on the same codebase, merge conflicts can arise. These conflicts occur when two or more people make changes to the same part of a file.

Identifying Merge Conflicts:

- Conflict Markers: Git will add special markers to the conflicting files, indicating the conflicting sections.
- Error Messages: Git will display error messages indicating the files with conflicts.

Resolving Merge Conflicts:

1. Manual Resolution:
    - Open the conflicting files in a text editor.
    - Identify the conflicting sections, which will be marked with special markers.
    - Decide which changes to keep and which to discard.
    - Manually edit the files to resolve the conflicts.
2. Using a Merge Tool:
    - Many Git clients and IDEs have built-in merge tools that can help you visualize and resolve conflicts.
    - These tools often provide a graphical interface to compare changes and choose the desired outcome.

Resolving Conflicts in the Command Line:

1. Stage the Resolved Files: Once you've resolved the conflicts, stage the files:

Bash

```
git add filename.txt
```

2. Commit the Merge: Commit the merge with a descriptive message:

Bash

git commit -m "Merged feature-branch with conflict resolution"

Preventing Merge Conflicts:

- Frequent Merging: Merge your branches regularly to minimize the risk of large conflicts.
- Small, Focused Commits: Make smaller, more focused commits to reduce the likelihood of conflicts.
- Clear Communication: Communicate with your team members to coordinate work and avoid overlapping changes.
- Use a Branching Strategy: A well-defined branching strategy can help you manage your branches effectively and reduce the risk of conflicts.

By understanding the process of resolving merge conflicts and following best practices, you can efficiently manage conflicts and maintain a clean Git history.

10.4 Code Review and Pull Requests

Code review is a critical process in software development that involves having another developer examine your code for errors, potential improvements, and adherence to coding standards. Pull requests are a mechanism for submitting code changes for review and merging.

The Code Review Process:

1. Create a Feature Branch: Create a new branch for the feature or bug fix you're working on.

2. Commit Changes: Commit your changes to the branch.
3. Push the Branch: Push your branch to a remote repository.
4. Create a Pull Request: Submit a pull request to the main branch, describing the changes made.
5. Code Review: Other developers review the code, providing feedback and suggestions.
6. Address Feedback: Make necessary changes based on the feedback.
7. Merge the Pull Request: Once the code is approved, the pull request is merged into the main branch.

Best Practices for Code Review:

- Clear and Concise Commit Messages: Write clear and concise commit messages that explain the purpose of the changes.
- Well-Formatted Code: Adhere to coding standards and use consistent formatting.
- Thorough Testing: Test your code thoroughly before submitting a pull request.
- Constructive Feedback: Provide constructive feedback, focusing on the code, not the person.
- Timely Reviews: Review pull requests promptly and provide feedback in a timely manner.
- Use a Code Review Tool: Use a code review tool like GitHub's pull request feature or a dedicated code review tool to facilitate the review process.

Benefits of Code Review:

- Improved Code Quality: Identifies and fixes bugs and potential issues early in the development process.
- Knowledge Sharing: Promotes knowledge sharing and collaboration among team members.
- Enforced Coding Standards: Ensures that code adheres to established standards and guidelines.

- Reduced Technical Debt: Helps prevent the accumulation of technical debt.

By effectively utilizing code review and pull requests, you can improve the quality of your code, enhance team collaboration, and deliver high-quality software.

Chapter 11: Best Practices for Git

11.1 Writing Good Commit Messages

A well-written commit message is essential for maintaining a clear and understandable project history. Good commit messages make it easier to review code changes, track down issues, and collaborate with other developers.

Key Guidelines for Writing Good Commit Messages:

1. Be Clear and Concise:
    - Use clear and concise language.
    - Avoid jargon and unnecessary details.
    - Focus on the core changes made.
2. Use the Imperative Mood:
    - Write commit messages as if you're giving commands.
    - For example, "Fix bug in login functionality" instead of "Fixed bug in login functionality."
3. Start with a Strong Subject Line:
    - The first line should be a concise summary of the change.
    - Use a 50-character limit for the subject line.
4. Provide a Detailed Description:
    - The following lines should provide more context and details about the changes.
    - Explain the "why" and "how" of the changes.
5. Use the Present Tense:
    - Write commit messages in the present tense.

Example of a Good Commit Message:

Fix bug in login functionality

This commit fixes a bug where users were unable to log in if their password

contained special characters. The issue was caused by a missing escape

character in the password validation regex.

Additional Tips:

- Use a Consistent Style: Maintain a consistent style for your commit messages.
- Avoid Vague Commit Messages: Avoid generic messages like "Fix bugs" or "Update code."
- Break Down Large Commits: If a commit is too large, break it down into smaller, more focused commits.
- Use a Commit Message Template: Consider using a template to ensure consistency and completeness.

By following these guidelines, you can write clear, concise, and informative commit messages that will benefit your team and future contributors.

11.2 Keeping Your Commit History Clean

A clean and well-organized commit history is essential for effective collaboration and maintainability. Here are some tips for keeping your commit history clean:

1. Write Clear and Concise Commit Messages:

- Use clear and concise language to describe the changes made in each commit.
- Avoid vague or generic messages.

- Use the imperative mood (e.g., "Fix bug in login functionality").

2. Use Small, Focused Commits:

- Break down large changes into smaller, more focused commits.
- Each commit should ideally address a single issue or feature.
- This makes it easier to review changes, revert to previous versions, and understand the project history.

3. Rebase Your Branches:

- Rebase your feature branches onto the main branch before merging.
- This helps to keep the main branch's history linear and clean.
- However, be cautious when rebasing shared branches, as it can cause conflicts.

4. Squash Commits:

- Use the git rebase -i command to squash multiple small commits into a single commit.
- This can help to clean up your commit history and make it more readable.

5. Use Interactive Rebase:

- The git rebase -i command allows you to reorder, edit, or squash commits.
- Use this feature to clean up your commit history and make it more logical.

6. Avoid Committing Unnecessary Changes:

- Only commit changes that are necessary to the current feature or bug fix.

- Avoid committing unnecessary files or changes that are not related to the current work.

7. Use a Consistent Style:

- Use a consistent style for your commit messages, code formatting, and other coding practices.
- This makes it easier to read and understand your code.

By following these guidelines, you can maintain a clean and well-organized commit history, which will benefit you and your team in the long run.

11.3 Effective Branching Strategies

A well-defined branching strategy is crucial for efficient and organized software development. It helps manage different development phases, collaborate with team members, and maintain a clean and understandable project history.

Here are some popular branching strategies:

1. Feature Branch Workflow

- Create a New Branch: Create a new branch for each feature or bug fix.
- Develop the Feature: Work on the feature on the new branch.
- Merge the Branch: Once the feature is complete, merge the branch into the main branch.
- Delete the Branch: Delete the feature branch after merging.

2. Gitflow Workflow

- Main Branch: The primary branch for production-ready code.
- Develop Branch: The main development branch.

- Feature Branches: Created from the develop branch for specific features.
- Release Branches: Created from the develop branch to prepare for a release.
- Hotfix Branches: Created from the main branch to fix urgent bugs.

3. Forking Workflow

- Fork the Repository: Create a personal copy of the main repository.
- Create a Feature Branch: Create a new branch in your forked repository.
- Develop the Feature: Work on the feature on the new branch.
- Push Changes: Push your changes to your forked repository.
- Create a Pull Request: Submit a pull request to the main repository.

Best Practices for Branching:

- Clear and Descriptive Branch Names: Use clear and concise names for your branches.
- Frequent Merging: Merge your branches regularly to avoid conflicts.
- Rebase Feature Branches: Rebase your feature branches onto the main branch before merging to keep the history clean.
- Delete Unnecessary Branches: Clean up your repository by deleting unnecessary branches.
- Use a Branching Strategy: Choose a branching strategy that suits your team's needs and project complexity.

By following these best practices and choosing an appropriate branching strategy, you can effectively manage your Git workflow, collaborate with your team, and deliver high-quality software.

11.4 Using Git for Team Projects

Git is an invaluable tool for collaborative software development. When used effectively, it can streamline workflows, improve code quality, and enhance team productivity.

Key Strategies for Effective Team Collaboration with Git:

1. Centralized Repository:

- Shared Repository: Establish a central repository on a platform like GitHub, GitLab, or Bitbucket.
- Remote Access: Grant team members access to the repository.
- Regular Synchronization: Encourage team members to regularly push their changes to the remote repository.

2. Branching Strategy:

- Feature Branches: Create separate branches for each feature or bug fix.
- Main Branch: Use a main branch for stable, production-ready code.
- Development Branch: Use a development branch for ongoing development.
- Merge Requests: Use pull requests to review and merge changes.

3. Code Review:

- Establish a Review Process: Set up a process for code reviews, specifying who reviews code and when.
- Provide Constructive Feedback: Offer specific feedback on code quality, style, and functionality.
- Iterative Review: Use an iterative review process to improve code quality.

4. Conflict Resolution:

- Merge Conflicts: Resolve merge conflicts promptly and efficiently.
- Communication: Communicate with team members to avoid conflicts or resolve them quickly.
- Merge Tools: Use merge tools to visualize and resolve conflicts.

5. Best Practices:

- Clear Commit Messages: Write concise and informative commit messages.
- Frequent Commits: Commit changes frequently to avoid large, complex commits.
- Regularly Push Changes: Push changes to the remote repository regularly to keep it up-to-date.
- Use a Git Workflow: Adopt a suitable workflow like Gitflow or a simpler workflow for your team's needs.
- Leverage Git Tools: Use Git tools like git log, git diff, and git bisect to analyze and debug code.
- Continuous Integration and Continuous Delivery (CI/CD): Implement CI/CD pipelines to automate testing, building, and deployment.

By following these best practices and effectively utilizing Git's features, teams can collaborate efficiently, improve code quality, and streamline their development processes.

Appendix

A.1 Troubleshooting Common Git Issues

Common Git Issues and Solutions:

1. Merge Conflicts:
   - Identify Conflicts: Git will highlight the conflicting sections in your files.
   - Resolve Conflicts: Manually edit the files to resolve the conflicts.
   - Stage Resolved Files: Stage the resolved files using git add.
   - Commit the Merge: Commit the merged changes.
2. Accidental Commits:
   - Undo Staging: Use git reset HEAD <file> to unstage a file.
   - Undo a Commit: Use git reset --soft HEAD~1 to move the HEAD pointer to the previous commit without changing the staging area.
3. Lost Changes:
   - Check the Reflog: Use git reflog to see a history of recent actions, including discarded commits.
   - Recover Changes: Use git checkout <commit-hash> -- <file> to recover a specific file from a previous commit.
4. Remote Repository Issues:
   - Verify Remote URL: Use git remote -v to check the remote URL.
   - Update Remote: Use git remote update to fetch the latest information from the remote repository.
   - Push Changes: Use git push origin <branch-name> to push your changes to the remote repository.
5. Branching and Merging Problems:

- Visualize Branches: Use tools like git log --graph --oneline --decorate to visualize the branch history.
  - Rebase Carefully: Use git rebase to clean up your commit history, but be cautious as it can rewrite history.
  - Merge Strategically: Choose the appropriate merge strategy (fast-forward or merge commit) based on the branch relationship.

General Troubleshooting Tips:

- Use git status: Check the status of your repository to understand the current state.
- Consult the Git Documentation: Refer to the official Git documentation for detailed information and solutions.
- Search Online: Many Git-related issues have been discussed and solved online.
- Experiment with Git Commands: Experiment with different Git commands to find solutions to specific problems.
- Seek Help: Ask questions on forums like Stack Overflow or GitHub.

By understanding these common Git issues and their solutions, you can effectively troubleshoot problems and maintain a clean and efficient Git workflow.

A.2 Git Cheat Sheet

Basic Commands

- git init: Initialize a new Git repository.
- git clone <url>: Clone an existing repository.
- git add <file>: Add a file to the staging area.
- git add .: Add all files to the staging area.
- git commit -m "message": Commit changes with a message.
- git status: Check the current status of the repository.

- git diff: Show differences between commits, files, or branches.
- git log: Show commit history.
- git log --oneline --graph --decorate: Show a concise, graphical log.
- git show <commit-hash>: Show details of a specific commit.

Branching and Merging

- git branch <branch-name>: Create a new branch.
- git checkout <branch-name>: Switch to a specific branch.
- git checkout -b <branch-name>: Create and[1] switch to a new branch.
- git merge <branch-name>: Merge the specified branch into the current branch.
- git rebase <branch-name>: Rebase the current branch onto the specified branch.

Remote Repositories

- git remote add <name> <url>: Add a remote repository.
- git fetch <remote>: Fetch changes from a remote repository.
- git pull <remote> <branch>: Fetch and merge changes from a remote branch.
- git push <remote> <branch>: Push changes to a remote repository.

Other Useful Commands

- git reset --hard HEAD~1: Undo the last commit.
- git revert <commit-hash>: Create a new commit that reverses a specific commit.
- git cherry-pick <commit-hash>: Apply a specific commit to a different branch.
- git stash: Temporarily save changes.

- git stash pop: Restore the most recently stashed changes.

Tips and Tricks

- Use Git Aliases: Create shortcuts for frequently used commands.
- Learn Interactive Rebase: Use git rebase -i to edit the commit history.
- Use a Good Git GUI: Tools like GitKraken or SourceTree can simplify complex operations.
- Experiment and Learn: Don't be afraid to experiment and learn from mistakes.
- Consult the Documentation: Refer to the official Git documentation for detailed information.

By mastering these Git commands and best practices, you can effectively manage your projects and collaborate with others.

www.ingramcontent.com/pod-product-compliance
Ingram Content Group UK Ltd.
Pitfield, Milton Keynes, MK11 3LW, UK
UKHW051648190125
4173UKWH00052B/3187